BILYANA

Thank you, God, for guiding me, providing for me, and blessing me all these years.

To my parents (†), brothers, and sister, for their unconditional love.
To Narya, for always encouraging me to move forward. To my pastors
Titus and Evi, who have lovingly helped me grow in faith and understand
life's purpose. To my aunt Kian, for her endless love and caring.

To Yasuo and Cindy, who kindly opened many doors to make this book happen.

To all my team—Rosie, Nenny (†),Waty, Ester, Boy, Syelvia, Yenny, Cicilia,
Fanny, Cing, Tess, Hadi, Ivonne, Mulyana, Ivony, Imam, Lily, Nenny, Frida,
Sherly, Yuri, Frans, Levi, Dini, Christine, Erna, Retno, Evi, Ketut, Yunin,
and Serenus—whose generous efforts have helped me make all the beautiful
things we believe in.

And, finally, to everyone who has had such faith in my designs and me.

BIYAN

Edited by
MARC ASCOLI

Interviewed by
NATASHA FRASER-CAVASSONI

RIZZOLI
NEW YORK

New York · Paris · London · Milan

*Soul and emotion—
these are important.*

Biyan Wanaatmadja

*I have long devoted myself
to the creation of beautiful things,
exploring every element of design
and trying to find new discoveries
in age-old traditions and fabrics.*

*This book is a continuation of that goal
and, much like a conversation,
it permits me to share my ideas and
deeply held beliefs.*

BIYAN WANAATMADJA

IN CONVERSATION

A DISCUSSION BETWEEN BIYAN WANAATMADJA
& NATASHA FRASER-CAVASSONI

Natasha: *Does the archetypal Biyan woman exist?*

Biyan: When I design, I don't think about myself but instead the woman I have in mind, and how my designs will look on her or how she will wear or mix pieces to make them her own.

N *What is your main intention concerning your designs?*

B It has always been my wish to be able to make a design that is beautiful, unique, and personal—something that will evolve with the wearer and where balance is key, as that reflects the woman and her choice.

N *Does it matter how a woman feels in your clothes?*

B It has always been my desire to see women happy wearing my designs, and especially to see how they put the elements together in their own personal styles.

N *Every detail counts, doesn't it?*

B Absolutely. To be involved in what I do requires certain responsibilities for which I have no choice but to care about every detail. I have tried to create a personal and intimate enterprise. Perhaps that explains my surge of excitement about each design—and I'm referring to all aspects of design. It's all about the process.

N *Describe designing a collection.*

B Every stage of my work is an experience in which my team and I share, discuss, and learn from each other as we explore and discover new things. I feel the more you know about fashion, the more you realize there is still so much left to learn. It's essential to keep open-minded and authentic when adapting designs to a woman's lifestyle.

N *How many people work for you directly?*

B There are about thirty people working in the atelier, including design assistants, pattern designers, and textile and graphic designers, as well as embroidery and beading specialists. Some of them are young and I love their energy and enthusiasm. We are like a family, as we have been working together for several years.

N *Were you involved in their hiring?*

B I always try to be present at the first interview. Hiring someone is all about instinct and chemistry. Finding and blending the right positive dynamics are very important processes in fostering a studio's atmosphere. Of course, it matters to have someone talented but I am more drawn by a person's character and energy.

N *How many collections do you design a year?*

B We do two collections a year for our presentation in the Paris showroom, Autumn-Winter in January and Spring-Summer in July. We have our once-a-year fashion show in Jakarta for the Spring-Summer season.

N *How long does each collection take?*

B It takes between five and six months, starting with investigating a mood, finding the story and direction, and experimenting with patterns and proportions, as well as exploring details and motifs by mixing, clashing, or juxtaposing elements to find the right ingredients. It is indeed an ongoing and interesting process, and one that I enjoy.

N *Do you get nervous before your fashion shows?*

B It always feels the same: a combination of excitement and curiosity but also anxiety. I feel self-assured but uncertain at the same time. The more I think about it, the more anxious I get—that never changes. Certain people say, "But you've done your show so many times, you must be used to it." But no, my stage nerves never diminish.

N *Do you remember your first fashion show in 1988?*

B Yes, I had exactly the same mix of feelings.

N *Being born in Surabaya suggests an exotic background.*

B Both of my parents lived through the war that led to Indonesia's independence in 1945. I was born in 1954, when their circumstances had improved. They ran a plastics manufacturing business while raising four children. I was the youngest in the family by nine years.

N *It sounds as if you were brought up like an only child.*

B My childhood was a happy one. My father was a calm and quiet man while my mother was the opposite. She was strong and more outspoken on certain occasions. They were both loving but didn't believe in handing out praise. Paying too many compliments was not how they functioned.

N *Is that typical for Indonesians?*

B The Chinese-Indonesians can be more reserved and undemonstrative. To a certain extent, it prepares you for life and encourages a kind of drive.

N *Your childhood sounded strict.*

B It was disciplined yet it also managed to be very cozy. Both of my parents were brought up during the Dutch colonial period, which led to Dutch being spoken to all their children as well as Indonesian and Javanese. In general, respect for the elderly is a very important principle in our family life. We had a ritual of visiting other family members during prominent holidays like Christmas, New Year, and the Chinese New Year.

N *Did you wear white as a child because of the heat?*

B I went to a Christian school and white was the color of my school uniform; its impression of discipline and unity is something I will never forget.

N *You have a way with white that is very special.*

B I perceived white as a symbol of purity since an early age. Only as I grew older did I become aware that there are many tones in white.

N *How would you describe your family home?*

B We lived in a simple, light-filled Dutch Colonial house. I never had my own bedroom; I shared one with my parents until I was six and thereafter I shared a room with my brother. That was typical for Indonesia.

N *How did you celebrate Christmas?*

B We always had a Christmas tree, delicious food, and a mix of Indonesian and Dutch traditions. It was always something to look forward to.

N *Did you do any sports?*

B Badminton used to be very popular during the time I was growing up but I wasn't really into it. To be honest, I wasn't that sporty. On one occasion, in fact, I almost drowned during my first swimming pool outing.

N *How?*

B It was during a school picnic when I was about six or seven. We went to a pool, and lots of my schoolmates were jumping in and swimming. It looked fun and easy and I simply followed them in . . . I realized that the more I panicked the more scared I became. It was my first scary moment.

N *Who saved you?*

B Nobody. Suddenly I just got out of the water and behaved as if nothing had happened.

N *Amazing. And you survived to tell the tale. With the hindsight of more than five decades, do you think it was the unknown that attracted you?*

B I'm not quite sure. . . . But when I travel, the unknown always appeals to me.

N *Explain your departure for Dusseldorf in 1973.*

B After my high school graduation in Surabaya, I was going to study at the university in Jakarta. But my mother suggested that I join my brother in Germany as I was going to leave home anyway. We are a very close-knit family and she wanted to make sure I was well looked after.

N *Germany must have been a shock.*

B I didn't know what to expect from European weather. It was cold and gray. It was a shock but it forced me to be independent. At home everything used to be provided for me, but in Dusseldorf I had to learn to stand on my own. My brother was a hardworking doctor and father of two young boys and he had his own hours and schedule so I had to become organized.

N *What were you doing?*

B I applied to be a dental student because I thought it was healthful and it had the added bonus of allowing me to work in a laboratory. But there was a quota for foreign students at that time and it was difficult to get into the program. So I ended up studying architecture for about two semesters.

N *How did your interest in fashion begin?*

B Almost every day after college, I dawdled in town, fascinated by the window displays of shops and boutiques. They really grabbed me; I guess the fashion bug hit me hard. My turning point came when my father passed away in 1975 and I had to return home. As if it were yesterday, I remember telling my mother, "I know what I want to do—I want to be in fashion." And she didn't say a word. Instead, she discussed my decision with trusted relatives.

N *What happened after that?*

B I returned to Dusseldorf and found a private fashion school, Müller & Sohn. It specializes in professional patternmaking, which is an excellent skill to have. I took a two-and-a-half-year course, and I also was an intern, so I worked part-time at a small company, doing all the basic tasks. The experience taught me about the need for quality, discipline, and good general organization in a fashion company.

N *Why did you apply to the London College of Fashion?*

B I wanted to know more about designing. I thought London would be the best place to study fashion because of its "street" energy, which is so rich and eclectic. At one moment, you'll see someone very proper and then at another, someone outrageous.

N *Due to Müller & Sohn, you skipped the first year of college and went directly into the second year, didn't you?*

B True. I have to say I got really frustrated during that year. Part of the course involved attending fashion shows and sketching the looks. Most of my classmates were so good and so fast at sketching. I tried to keep up with them but felt as though I was failing miserably.

N *How did the situation resolve itself?*

B Stephen Worth, one of my design tutors, noticed what I was going through. I asked him if I was good enough to do all this. He explained that each one of us was born with a certain gift: "If you draw a line, you can draw it straight but others can only draw it slanted. There is no right or wrong. Each of us can and should be unique."

N *Stephen Worth sounds like an excellent mentor.*

B He then asked me what I wanted to do—whether I was interested in fashion illustration or in making clothes. I said, "I want to make clothes." And he replied, "Don't worry about your sketches as long as you know how to explain what you need." And that was really the beginning of everything. It was an amazing moment.

N *When you were still a student, you got a job at Enrico Coveri. How did that come about?*

B Another of my design tutors, Michael Talboys, suggested that I go for an interview. During the interview, I admitted that I wasn't good at sketching, as I just wanted to be honest. But, surprisingly, I was hired.

N *What was the experience like?*

B It wasn't very long, only about four months. But it was my first time working in a fashion studio and it taught me about a studio's layout and the organization. Action-packed and intense, it also introduced me to other sides of the business: politics and intrigue.

N *Did you ever try to work in Paris?*

B Like everyone else starting out, Paris was my dream. I yearned to work in Paris because it is the city most closely linked to fashion, as simple as that. It wasn't easy, as fashion in Paris is highly competitive. Then in 1983 my mother asked me to come back home. I had been in Europe for ten years, so when I returned I didn't know what to do because I wasn't familiar with the industry.

N *So what happened?*

B I just started doing things by myself, cutting my own patterns and sourcing whatever fabrics were available. One day I was contacted by a magazine from Jakarta; they had heard that I'd been in Europe and trained at one of London's best fashion colleges. They asked if I would be interested in a photo shoot of my designs for an article in their magazine, which led to a lot of other opportunities. It was in 1985 that my career started.

N *In 1985, your career was given a major boost.*

B I was invited to attend Singapore Fashion Connection. The organization was keen to form a Southeast Asian platform, inviting designers from Indonesia, Thailand, Malaysia, the Philippines, Vietnam, and Singapore. The official brief was to design a collection that explored our seasons, environment, culture, and heritage. We were also part of a panel discussing the venture. It was both an important and necessary experience.

N *Why was it necessary?*

B It was necessary because my education in Europe had trained me for the aesthetic and practical side of the fashion industry. But then when I returned home to Indonesia, the modus operandi was completely different.

N *In what way?*

B During that time, everyone in fashion was into the thrill and excitement of new fabrication. But when I came home, nothing was centralized. Deciding to do something different meant researching and sourcing everything myself. Being invited by Singapore Fashion Connection gave me a true challenge.

N *Your Singapore experience forced you to be realistic about the situation.*

B My experience in Singapore became like a combination of my time in Europe and being close to home.

N *What did you want to do?*

B I wanted to explore and forge a new path for myself. Indonesia is known for its many and diverse traditional crafts, for example, batik, ikat, weaving, and hand embroidery—and these made me curious how I could incorporate this exquisite workmanship into something more contemporary. That said, I didn't know where to start. Then I remembered that my grandmother always wore the Peranakan style—a cultural cross between Chinese and Indonesian. It is very traditional, white-on-white embroidery or pastel on white. And all this was simply inspiring for me . . . and that was how it started.

N *Traditionally, Indonesian embroidery is beaded, isn't it?*

B Not always, as we have various kinds of embroidery, and they are all interesting and special to me. With that in mind I became more and more curious, exploring and experimenting in order to discover new possibilities.

N *How did the debut of your collection come about in 1988?*

B For that, I had to design about twenty-four looks in conjunction with the opening of a new hotel in Surabaya. The collection was simple and sleek.

N *Where were you making your clothes?*

B I started out with a small studio, together with an assistant and two seamstresses in my small garage. There we made our first collection.

N *You planted a seed.*

B Indeed, everything flows organically. I was tremendously interested in trying all kinds of different methods and processes.

N *Elaborate embroidery has become one of your signature elements. How many people have you trained in that domain?*

B I have no idea! When I started, there wasn't much demand for or interest in it. But through the years, as its beauty has become more recognized, many people have come to learn and work as embroiderers. Interest in it has grown since then.

N *Like everything in fashion, if you know what you want, you eventually get it. How has your embroidery developed?*

B I've always been fascinated by the intricate beadwork and beautiful embroidery of the past, as well as other forms of traditional craftsmanship, which have become important elements of my design.

N *Why do you like embroidery?*

B It's a kind of storytelling, and so exquisite. It's a skill that represents the character and circumstances of the maker, whether it's Chinese embroidery, Japanese kimono, or Indonesian batik and kebaya . . . all of which inspire me.

N *You have described embroidery as being mysterious.*

B In my experience, it always has an element of wait and see before getting the result—a case of "expect the unexpected" along with a mild surprise or two. Small swatches can look amazing, then after the design is incorporated, it can simply be too much or not enough. Everything in embroidery is about composition.

N *How would you define harmony, with regard to embroidery?*

B It is not always about perfection. It is about balance and emotion.

N *With your designs, you have taken embroidery and batik to another place. But when choosing fabrics, what are you after?*

B It's the richness and sensation of the fabric. I like something unique with a special composition that I can put together with different types of layering. Fabrics further the softness and refinement of a garment but still, out of respect for the women who wear the garments, a design has to function and be easy to wear.

N *Before we begin on your house and garden, does your pair of white peacocks screech?*

B They do, especially in the morning! But it is always pleasant to start the day hearing them sing and chirp. To me they represent the innocence of nature, especially when they are flying around the garden. It furthers the ambience.

N *And you have a dog . . .*

B His name is Zeus, and he is a little French bulldog.

N *In appearance, your house manages to evoke order and calm. Would you agree?*

B A home should reflect a sense of culture and spirituality, as well as everything the owner loves. To me, domestic tranquillity is very important. I spend almost twelve hours in the office, so when I return home, its calmness balances and neutralizes all the activities of my day. Sometimes I'm just happy to walk in, close the door, and feel relaxed. I realize also that it has become like a sanctuary to me, where I can have my intimate time with God.

N *Did you work with an architect to design your home?*

B I worked with Gregorius Supie Yolodi, a talented young architect. I liked his aesthetic and simplicity. To appoint an architect is equivalent to a partnership—the chemistry has to work.

N *Did you source local Indonesian materials?*

B We tried to use local materials as much as possible, such as Indonesian marble, stone, and wood. I especially love Indonesian teak; it adds warmth and depth to a home, and as it ages its patina looks even more beautiful.

N *How long did the house take to build?*

B It took two years.

N *What about the décor?*

B It is an ongoing process. A home has to resemble and complement you—call it a fusion of different but necessary energies. Interiors have to breathe and evolve with your moods. It is important to be able to play around with an interior and spend time tweaking it. I might wake up in the morning in the mood to adjust something, and then the next morning I might think, this is not what I want, and wonder what I've done. Decorating on your own leads to a fair amount of trial and error.

N *Who designed the garden?*

B I worked together with a landscape designer by giving ideas of what I would like to have in the garden.

N *Do you have a favorite view?*

B I like to sit at the back of the house, facing the garden with the morning sun—the sunlight soothes me. The verdure of the garden is calming and I like the idea of watching nature and sensing different types of life.

N *Your personal collection of necklaces suggests patience. Are you patient by nature?*

B Collecting those necklaces required patience as they had to be discovered all over Indonesia. But that was part of the excitement: researching, desiring, and then acquiring. Often the most beautiful things are hard to find and demand time and patience.

N *What about in regards to your work?*

B I am both patient and impatient, probably like everyone else. That said, I am aware that the best result requires patience, and if you can't wait, the result isn't worth it. Pacing is important; some things take time and cannot be rushed, while other things have to be immediate. It's like the laws of nature.

N *How do you recharge? By nature, you're dutiful and so a lot must pile up on your plate.*

B Bali is a wonderful place to escape; it's only one and a half hours away. As soon as I arrived in Bali for the first time, I just knew that this was what I needed. It is a melting pot of wonders, cultures, and tranquility as well as being laidback, which is a pleasant change from my busy life in Jakarta.

N *When you are away, what do you miss about your home?*

B Mostly the home cooking and all the smells, like the Javanese tea, and of course my dog.

N *Your necklace collection is intriguing. It looks as though you own about sixty. When did that start?*

B I started collecting about fifteen years ago; some old pieces were bought from antique dealers. They originated from different places like Papua, Papua New Guinea, Timor, Sumba . . . some of them have fairy-tale stories behind them, such as one being a symbol of a marriage proposal.

N *Why do necklaces appeal to you?*

B I like the aesthetic of them, the rich depth of thought conveyed through their execution, and even the rawness of their materials.

N *Are there similarities between these necklaces and your work?*

B Perhaps they have many similarities because we want to create something that is not only beautifully crafted but capable of expressing the skills and emotions of the people who made it.

N *The necklaces remind me of your mood boards. When do you do the boards?*

B It's a process that begins with a creative meeting between my team and me before each collection, where we share and toss our ideas back and forth. These then become our initial guidelines.

N *Your collages are part of the same process, aren't they?*

B Yes, it's like putting in everything that we have in mind to share and to be discussed.

N *In only five years, you have created an international business. What do you think about that?*

B I always believe things happen for a reason. It's incredible how opportunities can arise. I dedicate my success to all the people I work with; to everyone who has believed in me all these years; and to Indonesia, the place where I was born, grew up, and have remained in my profession until today.

N *Your success overseas sounds like a double-edged sword.*

B In a way, it was a dream for me for the first twenty years. I took it as a very interesting exercise to keep improving and to better everything we do. However the downside— or rather the reality—is that maintaining our quality, especially when you make the brand globally available, requires a vast undertaking and responsibility to give your very best.

N *What drives you?*

B Intuition and passion.

N *It's been almost thirty years. A final thought about that?*

B It's only by His Grace.

*Embroidery has a long tradition
but remains subtle,
intense—even mysterious.*

ENCHANTED
TALES

The color blue never tires my eye.
It has a certain masculinity
that is contemporary and classic.

JAKARTA

JAKARTA

*Jakarta equals chaos
and energy . . .
but it's also the place
I call home.*

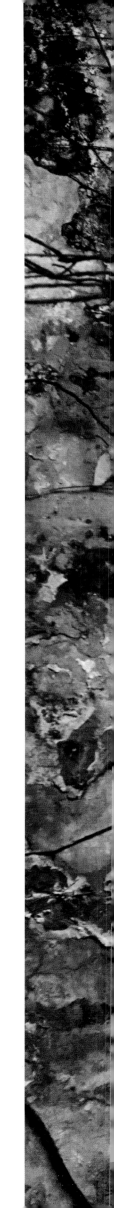

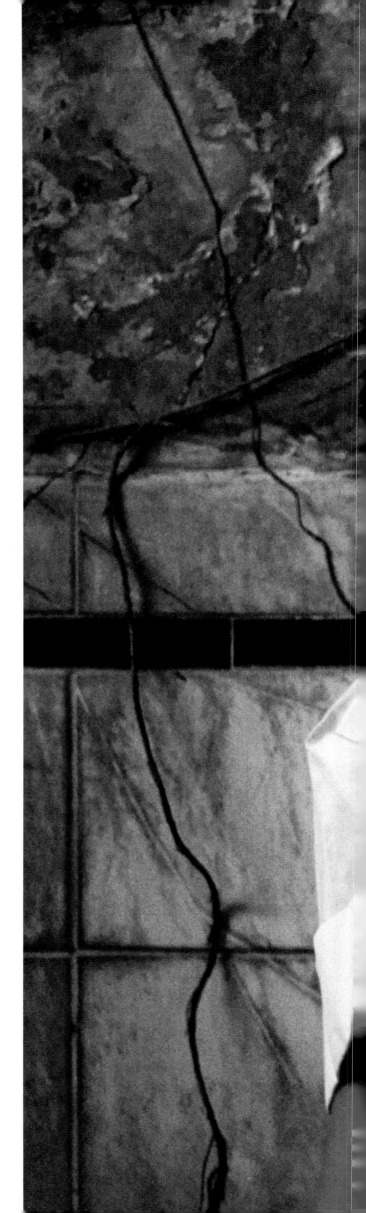

*I love necklaces
that convey complex
ideas and emotions.*

101

*Copper is understated
and ethereal.*

Flowers — at whatever stage of their lives — have a kind of sensuality.

DEVOTED

*I like the word "workmanship"
because it implies a process.*

Embroidery is storytelling brimming over with detail and emotion.

Organza
silk
ribbon 5mm x2

(A) type 10

BACKSTAGE

Moments before a show,
I feel a mix of fear,
excitement, and fulfillment.

It's a collaboration — the choice of models, makeup, and hair also helps to capture a collection's spirit.

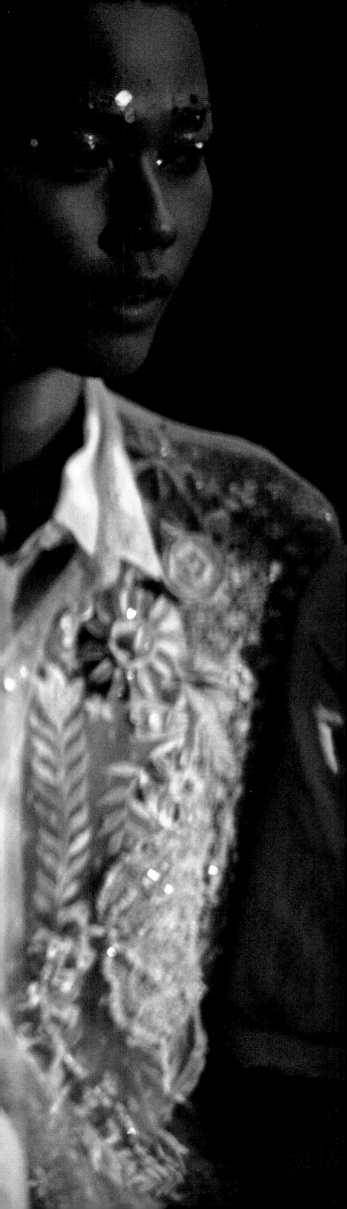

*I've worked with Rizal
for many years — he's one of the essential
elements behind every show.*

STARK
SIMPLICITY

A crane symbolizes happiness.
As a motif, whether applied or embroidered,
it has allure.

This neckline gives
a certain kind of grace.

PARIS
LA NUIT

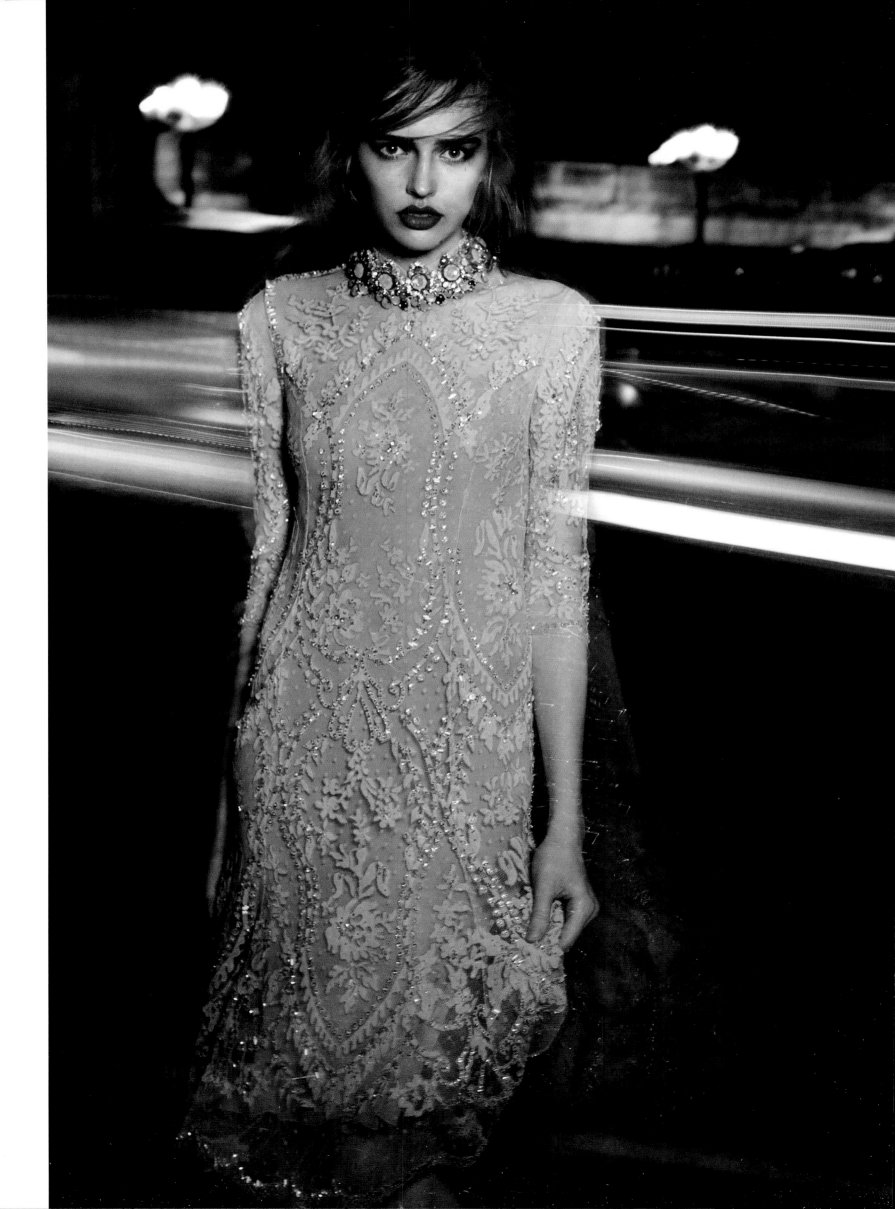

Paris, always changing,
seems dreamlike for that reason.

*All my designs evolve
with the wearer.*

MY
HOME

*Zeus, my loyal and
affectionate French bulldog.*

Exquisite ecclesiastical craftsmanship is an endless source of inspiration.

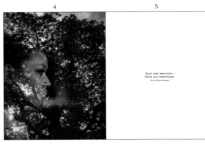

Spring-Summer 2014 collection, Bali
photograph by Davy Linggar

Biyan Wanaatmadja, Bali, 2013
photograph by Davy Linggar

Biyan's parents' wedding, Surabaya, 1936
Biyan and his father, Surabaya, 1956
Biyan and his brothers, Surabaya, 1959
photographs: all rights reserved

Biyan and his brothers and sister, Surabaya, 1956
Biyan, Amsterdam, 1979
photographs: all rights reserved

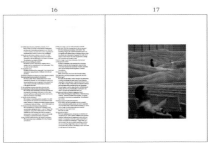

Biyan at the rehearsal before the show,
Spring-Summer 2008 collection, Jakarta
photograph by Davy Linggar

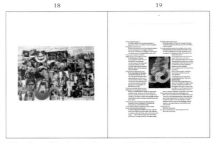

Mood board for Spring-Summer 2011 collection, Jakarta
photograph by Davy Linggar

A primitive Papuan necklace from Biyan's private collection
photograph by Davy Linggar

Mood board for Spring-Summer 2014 collection,
Jakarta

photographs: all rights reserved

Spring-Summer 2014 collection, Bali
photograph by Davy Linggar

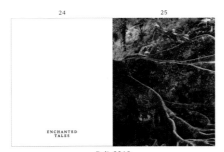

Bali, 2013
photograph by Davy Linggar

Bali, 2013
photograph by Stefan Khoo

Spring-Summer 2007 collection, Bali
(dress courtesy of Tania Tjiptobiantoro)
photograph by Stefan Khoo

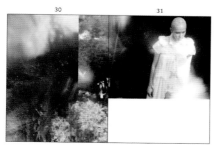

Bali, 2013
photograph by Stefan Khoo

Spring-Summer 2007 collection, Bali
(dress courtesy of Tania Tjiptobiantoro)
photograph by Stefan Khoo

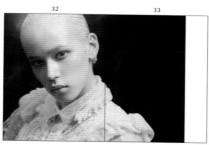

Spring-Summer 2007 collection, Bali
(dress courtesy of Tania Tjiptobiantoro)
photograph by Stefan Khoo

Spring-Summer 2014 collection, Bali
photograph by Stefan Khoo

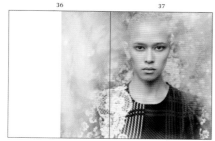

Spring-Summer 2014 collection, Bali
photograph by Stefan Khoo

Bali, 2013
photograph by Davy Linggar

Spring-Summer 2014 collection, Bali
photograph by Davy Linggar

Bali, 2013
photograph by Davy Linggar

Bali, 2013
photograph by Stefan Khoo

Spring-Summer 2014 collection, Bali
photograph by Davy Linggar

Bali, 2013
photograph by Davy Linggar

Bali, 2013
photograph by Davy Linggar

Spring-Summer 2007 collection, Bali
photographs by Davy Linggar and Stefan Khoo

Spring-Summer 2014 collection, Bali
photographs by Davy Linggar

Bali, 2013
photographs by Davy Linggar

Bali, 2013
photographs by Stefan Khoo

Spring-Summer 2014 collection, Bali
photograph by Stefan Khoo

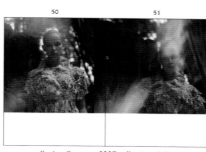

Spring-Summer 2007 collection, Bali
(embroidered coat courtesy of Tania Tjiptobiantoro)
photographs by Stefan Khoo

Bali, 2013
photographs by Davy Linggar

Spring-Summer 2014 collection, Bali
photographs by Davy Linggar

Spring-Summer collection 2014, Bali
photographs by Stefan Khoo

Bali, 2013
photograph by Stefan Khoo

Spring-Summer 2014 collection, Bali
photograph by Stefan Khoo

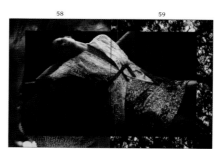

Top – Spring-Summer 2014 collection, Bali
Skirt – Spring-Summer 2010 collection, Bali
(sequinned skirt courtesy of Arulita Adityaswara)
photographs by Davy Linggar and Stefan Khoo

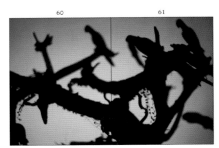

Bali, 2013
photograph by Davy Linggar

Spring-Summer 2014 collection, Bali
photograph by Davy Linggar

Bali, 2013
photograph by Davy Linggar

Spring-Summer 2014 collection, Bali
photograph by Stefan Khoo

Spring-Summer 2014 collection, Bali
photographs by Davy Linggar and Stefan Khoo

Spring-Summer 2014 collection, Bali
photograph by Davy Linggar

Spring-Summer 2014 collection, Bali
photograph by Davy Linggar

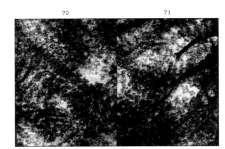

Bali, 2013
photograph by Davy Linggar

Spring-Summer 2014 collection, Bali
photograph by Stefan Khoo

Spring-Summer 2014 collection, Bali
photographs by Davy Linggar

Spring-Summer 2014 collection, Bali
photograph by Davy Linggar

Spring-Summer 2014 collection, Bali
photograph by Davy Linggar

Spring-Summer 2014 collection, Bali
photograph by Stefan Khoo

Jakarta, 2013
photograph by Davy Linggar

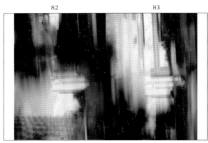

Jakarta, 2013
photographs by Davy Linggar

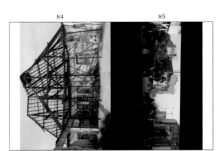

Jakarta, 2013
photographs by Davy Linggar

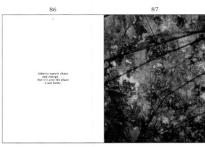

Jakarta, 2013
photograph by Stefan Khoo

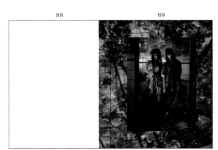

left — Spring-Summer 2008 collection, Jakarta
(sequinned dress courtesy of Tania Tjiptobiantoro)
right — Spring-Summer 2014 collection, Jakarta
photographs by Stefan Khoo

90 91

left – Spring-Summer 2008 collection, Jakarta
(dress courtesy of Tania Tjiptobiantoro)
right – Spring-Summer 2014 collection, Jakarta
photograph by Stefan Khoo

92 93

Spring-Summer 2012 collection, Jakarta
photograph by Stefan Khoo

94 95

Necklace – a primitive Papuan necklace from
Biyan's private collection
Top – Spring-Summer 2014 collection, Jakarta
photograph by Stefan Khoo

96 97

Spring-Summer 2014 collection, Jakarta
photograph by Stefan Khoo

98 99

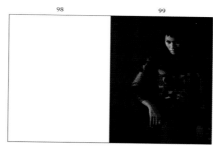

Spring-Summer 2014 collection, Jakarta
photograph by Stefan Khoo

100 101

Spring-Summer 2014 collection, Jakarta
photograph by Stefan Khoo

102 103

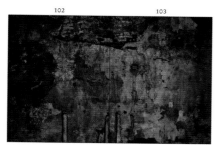

Jakarta, 2013
photograph by Stefan Khoo

104 105

Spring-Summer 2014 collection, Jakarta
photograph by Stefan Khoo

106 107

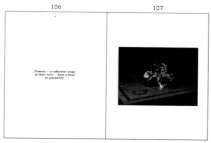

Jakarta, 2013
photograph by Stefan Khoo

108 109

Spring-Summer 2009 collection, Jakarta
photograph by Stefan Khoo

110 111

Spring-Summer 2014 collection, Bali
photograph by Davy Linggar

112 113

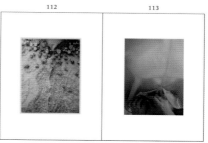

At the atelier, Jakarta, 2013
photographs by Davy Linggar

114 115

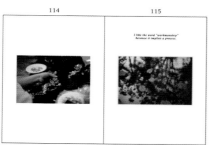

At the atelier, Jakarta, 2013
photograph by Davy Linggar

Bali, 2013
photograph by Davy Linggar

116 117

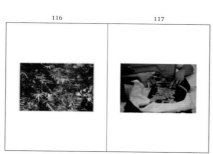

Jakarta, 2013
photograph by Davy Linggar

At the atelier, Jakarta, 2013
photograph by Davy Linggar

118 119

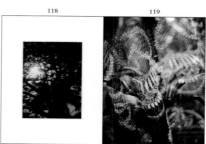

Bali, 2013
photograph by Davy Linggar

Spring-Summer 2014 collection, Bali
photograph by Davy Linggar

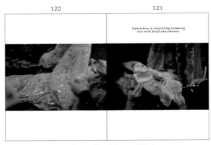

At the atelier, Jakarta, 2011
photograph by Davy Linggar

At the atelier, Jakarta, 2007
photograph by Davy Linggar

At the atelier, Jakarta, 2013
photograph by Davy Linggar

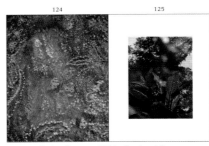

Spring-Summer 2014 collection, Jakarta
photograph by Davy Linggar

Bali, 2013
photograph by Davy Linggar

At the atelier, Jakarta, 2013
photograph by Davy Linggar

Spring-Summer 2014 collection, Jakarta
photograph by Davy Linggar

Spring-Summer 2014 collection, Jakarta
photograph by Davy Linggar

Spring-Summer 2009 collection, Jakarta
photograph by Davy Linggar

Textile exploration of Indonesian traditional
songket fabric from Palembang, Sumatra
photograph by Davy Linggar

Spring-Summer 2014 collection, Jakarta
photograph by Davy Linggar

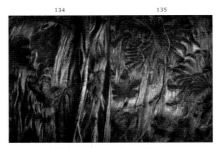

Cushion covers at home, Jakarta
photographs by Davy Linggar

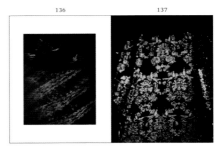

Textile exploration of Indonesian traditional
songket fabric from Palembang, Sumatra
photograph by Davy Linggar

Spring-Summer 2014 collection, Jakarta
photograph by Davy Linggar

Preparation before the show,
Spring-Summer 2013 collection, Jakarta
photograph by Davy Linggar

Spring-Summer 2013 collection, Jakarta
photograph by Davy Linggar

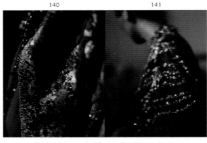

Spring-Summer 2011 collection, Jakarta
photographs by Davy Linggar

Spring-Summer 2014 collection, Jakarta
photograph by Davy Linggar

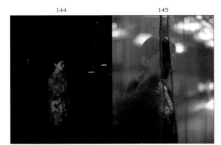

Before the show, Spring-Summer 2013 collection, Jakarta
photographs by Davy Linggar

Spring-Summer 2014 collection, Jakarta
photograph by Davy Linggar

Spring-Summer 2014 collection, Jakarta
photographs by Davy Linggar

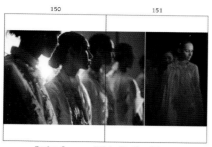

Spring-Summer 2014 collection, Jakarta
photograph by Hakim Satrio

Spring-Summer 2014 collection, Jakarta
photograph by Davy Linggar

Spring-Summer 2014 collection, Jakarta
photographs by Davy Linggar

Spring-Summer 2014 collection, Jakarta
photograph by Hakim Satrio

Spring-Summer 2014 collection, Jakarta
photograph by Hakim Satrio

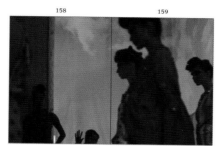

Spring-Summer 2010 collection, Jakarta
photograph by Davy Linggar

Spring-Summer 2010 collection, Jakarta
photograph by Davy Linggar

Spring-Summer 2014 collection, Jakarta
photograph by Davy Linggar

Spring-Summer 2011 collection, Jakarta
photograph by Davy Linggar

Rizal, the fashion show's director, Jakarta, 2011
photograph by Davy Linggar

Spring-Summer 2009 collection, Jakarta
photograph by Davy Linggar

Finale, Spring-Summer 2014 collection, Jakarta
photograph by Davy Linggar

Spring-Summer 2014 collection, Jakarta
photograph by Davy Linggar

Spring-Summer 2014 collection, Paris
photograph by Stefan Khoo

Spring-Summer 2014 collection, Paris
photographs by Stefan Khoo

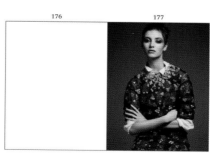

Spring-Summer 2014 collection, Paris
photograph by Stefan Khoo

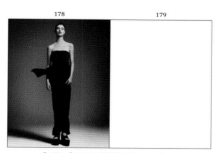

Spring-Summer 2009 collection, Paris
photograph by Stefan Khoo

180 181

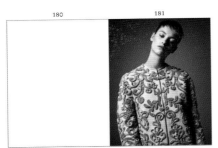

Spring-Summer 2009 collection, Paris
photograph by Stefan Khoo

182 183

Spring-Summer 2009 collection, Paris
(crane-embroidered kimono coat
courtesy of Arulita Adityaswara)
photograph by Stefan Khoo

184 185

Spring-Summer 2009 collection, Paris
(crane-embroidered kimono coat
courtesy of Arulita Adityaswara)
photograph by Stefan Khoo

186 187

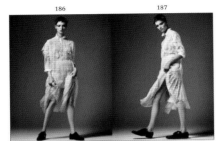

Spring-Summer 2014 collection, Paris
photographs by Stefan Khoo

188 189

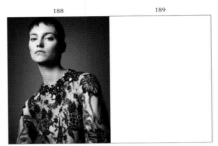

Spring-Summer 2014 collection, Paris
photograph by Stefan Khoo

190 191

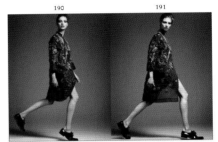

Spring-Summer 2014 collection, Paris
photographs by Stefan Khoo

192 193

Spring-Summer 2009 collection, Paris
photograph by Stefan Khoo

194 195

Spring-Summer 2014 collection, Paris
photograph by Stefan Khoo

196 197

Spring-Summer 2014 collection, Paris
photograph by Stefan Khoo

198 199

Spring-Summer 2014 collection, Paris
photograph by Stefan Khoo

200 201

Spring-Summer 2010 collection, Paris
photograph by Stefan Khoo

202 203

Spring-Summer 2010 collection, Paris
photograph by Stefan Khoo

204 205

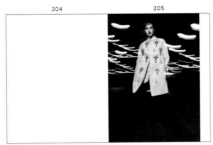

Spring-Summer 2014 collection, Paris
photograph by Stefan Khoo

206 207

Spring-Summer 2014 collection, Paris
photograph by Stefan Khoo

208 209

Spring-Summer 2014 collection, Paris
photograph by Stefan Khoo

At home, Jakarta, 2013
photograph by Davy Linggar

Balinese dog sculptures at home, Jakarta, 2013
photograph by Davy Linggar

At home, Jakarta, 2013
photograph by Davy Linggar

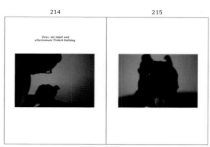

Jakarta, 2013
photograph by Davy Linggar

Zeus, Jakarta, 2013
photograph by Davy Linggar

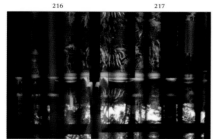

At home, Jakarta, 2013
photograph by Davy Linggar

Entrance at home, Jakarta, 2013
photograph by Davy Linggar

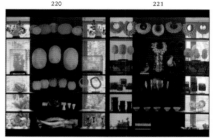

Collection of artifacts at home, Jakarta, 2013
photograph by Davy Linggar

Biyan's private collection of antique
Indonesian hair combs
photograph by Davy Linggar

At home, Jakarta, 2013
photograph by Davy Linggar

At home, Jakarta, 2013
photographs by Davy Linggar

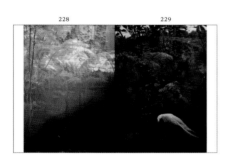

At home, Jakarta, 2013
photographs by Davy Linggar

The idea of creating a book first came to me because my fashion house's thirtieth anniversary was coming up, and, loving books, I wanted to make one for the occasion. But the book had to be more than a list of achieved goals. My aim was to make it about sharing experiences—and to make it as beautiful as possible.

I thought it was important to find someone who could help by seeing me from almost a detached point of view in order to bring something unexpected to the project. Yasuo Umetada, my friend and an associate of Marc Ascoli's, suggested him as art director. I particularly admire how his work always appears very contemporary and timeless. Marc has a unique aesthetic that is both poetic and elegant as well as that Parisian pursuit of quality that I understand and can identify with. A perfectionist, he can be quite intense and extremely demanding but he's someone who's easy to reason with.

The process entailed passionate discussions that led to an exchange of ideas and a fusion of chemistry and opinions. I introduced him to two excellent photographers whom I have been working with— Stefan Khoo from Singapore and Davy Linggar from Indonesia—which led to an amicable collaboration. In many ways, Marc's intuition is always one step ahead. He was right and consistent about everything on the project, from the organization of the chapters to the choice of writer, where, from the beginning, he only mentioned one name—Natasha Fraser-Cavassoni. Everything about this book—from its beginning to the end—has been the result of this unique combination of talents.

Thanks to

Agata Rudko
Alice Ghendrih
Ark Lin
Arulita Adityaswara
Boy Sembiring
Catherine Bonifassi
Chloé Berthaudin
Cicilia Fransisca
Cindy Ho
Dara Warganegara
Davy Linggar & his team
Diego Fellay
Ester Pasaribu
Frédérique Popet
Hakim Satrio
Hege Wollan
Iris Van Berne
Linsey Li
Neni Nuraini
Reti Ragil
Rosiani
Samudra Hartanto
Sebastien Richard
Stefan Khoo & his team
Suryawati
Syelvia
Tania Tjiptobiantoro
Tjahja Kusnadi
Vanessa Blondel
Yasuo Umetada
Yenny Mellisa

Very special thanks to

BANK NEGARA INDONESIA

First published in the United States of America in 2015
by Rizzoli International Publications, Inc.
300 Park Avenue South
New York, NY 10010
www.rizzoliusa.com

© 2015 Biyan
Interview: Natasha Fraser-Cavassoni

Edited by Marc Ascoli
Graphic Design: Atelier 32 – Diego Fellay & Chloé Berthaudin

Publisher: Charles Miers
Editorial Director: Catherine Bonifassi
Editor: Daniel Melamud
Production: Maria Pia Gramaglia and Kaija Markoe
Editorial Coordination: CASSI EDITION
Vanessa Blondel, Frédérique Popet

ISBN: 978-0-8478-4586-6
Library of Congress Control Number: 2014944057

Printed in China

2015 2016 2017 2018 / 10 9 8 7 6 5 4 3 2 1